A P
About
Shooting Stars

Daniel Kantak

Parson's Porch Books

A Rumor About Shooting Stars
ISBN: Softcover 978-1-955581-35-6
Copyright © 2021 by Daniel Kantak

Parson's Porch Books is an imprint of Parson's Porch *&* Company (PP*&*C) in Cleveland, Tennessee. PP*&*C is an innovative organization which raises money by publishing books of noted authors, representing all genres. Its face and voice is **David Russell Tullock** (dtullock@parsonsporch.com).

Parson's Porch *&* Company *turns books into bread & milk* by sharing its profits with the poor.

www.parsonsporch.com

A Rumor
About
Shooting Stars

Contents

A RUMOR ABOUT SHOOTING STARS

My father said that shooting stars
were new souls come down to earth.
I believed him until Mrs. Sweeny
my 5th grade teacher said, "Dan, what are meteorites."
I replied, "they are new souls come down to earth."
Mrs. Sweeny corrected me
with a nickel and iron rebuttal
that took my father's light away from me.
Never again did I hear
anyone even suggest
that shooting stars were
souls come down to earth.

So, here's your part in this.
The next time
you hear someone talking about meteorites,
please add
the rumor about the souls.

POTTER'S WHEEL

It is said
that the wet slap
of the potter's hand
upon a sphere of clay
sets the breath of life in it.
That the clay must be
drawn downward
then pulled upward
eleven times
before it finds its center upon the wheel.
That the firm open handed, loose-lock
of palm and fingers
surrounding it,
urging it upward
in the eleventh pulling
is its birth crowning.
That the clay knows more about the potter
than the potter knows of the clay.
That on days
when there is love in the potter's heart
the throw of a pot
is a wet sweet kiss
and warbled whisper.
That on days
when there is pain in the potter's heart
the throw of a pot
is a wearisome wobble
of off-centered thought.
That when truth comes to her crucible
and the pot is handed into the fire
there is no telling
if she will be taken
into purpose or into pieces
or how smoke will be written
into her glaze.

WATCHING SCULLS

When I was a boy
my father would drive
into North Syracuse
and we would roll up
the windows
through Solvay
on the shores of Onondaga
to help prevent
the foul stink
and fumes
from blistering smoke
smudging the air
like a crematorium
post- mortem.

World War Two
had left its
industrialized thumb print
in the crucible
of steel mills,
chemical industry.

Solvay Process
A chemical plant
known throughout
the Northeast
for its soda ash
stood
canker-lipping
a topography
white as sea gull droppings.
Mountainous ash heaps
upon barges
bound for
the lake's heart
to dump absolute waste
into Syracuse's sewer.

Over this moonscape
across cyanotic water
rowing races were held.

Putrid air
filled our lungs
as we watched sculls.

LAKE CHARLES

Lake Charles drank us.
Drank deep drafts of us
in the slalom of our escape
from merciless Louisiana summer.
We were Cypress in water
our roots tapping blind youth,
dropping a ski
one foot in front of the other
into the deep cut of
of seemingly perfect vitality.
What did we know
of fish rising breathless
under the wake
of our going
asphyxiated by
the toxicity of
vinyl chloride, benzene,
dioxins, and cadmium corruption,
of the mindless machine?
The crucible of chemical plants
that set bread upon our tables,
smokey bourbon in our glasses
—the plants that gave us light
gave us a harder darkness
shading our genetics
as mildew in grout between tiles.
We lived the dream
and woke up in the nightmare
of vague aches, cancer, birth defects,
the myalgia of chronic fatigue,
asymptomatic depression,
and a two-car garage.

CYPRESS TREE

With beards of moss the Cypress seem
a gathering of old men kibitzing.
Egret white, their hair is tossed,
a rookery of wings above what's mossed.
In the guttural throat thump that they sigh to
they stand and watch the murky bayou.
Blackened water can not defeat
those who have learned to soak their feet.
Nor sun burn down hot despair
who wear egrets in their hair.
Age seems a small pirogue
tethered to them bow to toe.
When I am old, and moss hangs me
I hope to be the cypress tree.

ARROYO DRUMMING

No water—but drums now—this silent channel.
A gully of beatings upon drumhead.
A wash of soul and ancient people's song.
That is no echo which beats back
but the lamentations of those who walk
slow in time—their charm of immortality
a breath of stars, a scorpion's tail.
Slower than the frost
they walk—each step, a hundred years.
Snakes rattle under their step.
And we a year in their moment
pass as a shooting star—then gone
into an infinity of ore.
Turn slow and see them now
between a blink and drum,
drum,
d
r
u
m.

KOOTZNOOWOO

(Fortress of the Bears)

Coastal Brown Bear,
grizzly salmon eater,
omnivore of temperate rainforest,
u-shaped valleys, and rounded ridge,
when the Tlinket took one of you
they covered your body with goose down
as a sign of peace
and pointed your head
in a certain way
so, your spirit would tell the other bears
that you had been treated with respect and honor.
Prickly porcupine ginseng (Devils Club)
Salmon berries red
and the Doppler shift of season sound,
Go round of rainforest green, green,
and green; and rain and rivulet white cascade,
muskeg and mountain stone scouring slip
hap dance return to source
in geometry of long nights, auroras,
and of brother salmons gift enough for all.

Where bears have walked
so many thousands of years
that the rock has become track,
this sacred place
Kootznoowoo,
fortress of the bears.

14

BLACK BEAR

Bear, I saw you
first among
Skunk Cabbage
yellow rainforest
crocus organ to sun;
fiddlehead ferns,
arpeggio of
nubile green innocence
curling upward
under your paws;
then Devil's Club
white flower bloom
of early summer bouquet
come to wedding
with Lupine bridesmaids
dressed in violet, pink
and deep purple
petal gowns;
then with dandelions;
you spent the summer
in meadows above
streams waiting
for salmon to
rush red with lifeblood
twisting, splashing
spun of spawn
to fill your belly
as fireweed
pink-purple troops
flanked summer
into her surrender.
Now you hibernate
in that memory;
curled in hollow
stump of fallen
spruce;
semi-oblivious

to relentless
gray granular
wind.

MAPLING

(So many years ago, my father would go mapling, tapping the sprawling leaf naked maple trees for sap. And I remember a few cords of wood next to the sugar shack and the mad steam rising from boiling sap cauldron. There is nothing sweeter in this world than white maple candy and its crystalline body.)

Sap buckets hung off
the gray-black-barked maples
 spring sweet sugaring
when long ago my father hung
buckets under taps he had drilled
into maple heart through white frost
of perfectly cool nights—warming days;
spring's persnickety proposal.
And into those buckets
dripped thick yellow sap
rebirth for boiling.
After reduction, filtering;
then
  short
  stack
  of
  summer.

CATFISH

You said that dad
always liked to take you fishing.
You had the patience
to sit and wait and watch.
Crowds of words
didn't chatter in your head
and the squawk of crows
was enough to settle
your need for language.
Your landscape was rural
—as factual as a barbed hook.
Your talent was observation
and from the fishing camp
in upward look
you knew every girder
and rivet in Bonnie's Bridge.
The low drone of tires
biting into the grate
of bridge road plate
were notes in your margins
of ring- worn cylinders
and asbestos brakes,
raining down fiber and fume
into your lungs.
And the tart, purple black
of the elderberry growing wild
in the shrub and brush
behind you set upon
your plate the small
hard seed of being.
You spit washed the world.
And the lines of slender death
that you and dad
cast out held a spell
into the river
conjuring
the

18

channel cat.
I remember you telling me
how you once closed your eyes
and saw a whiskered leviathan
coming up through the mud and silt.
And how you leapt up
expecting to hear
a reel go screaming
and see a flash of hands
grab a pole to set the hook
—but there was only dad,
bottle fallen from his hand
mumbling to himself
something about the war;
and you settled back
to watch rainbows
in thin film of oil floating by
from dump of barge bilge water;
being was enough for you,
you had no apprenticeship
in the shop of asking why.
When evening
settled out of light
your play was
the snapping of the fire
and the certain beauty of the stars;
and without a word
you would crawl
into the bed
of the old pickup
and sleep and dream
of barges with their deep draft
sucking the river under them,
revealing the slope
of shore to channel;
and of the long wide throat
which swallows everything,
the infinite gullet
of the Channel Cat.

And you would headless turn
in the Sleepy Hollow
of your hard bed
and see in swirls and eddies
of consciousness
the yellowing pages of years
drift under the bridge,
and your children born,
and grandpa,
and grandma,
and dad,
and mom,
and your beloved Uncle Carl.
wrapped in the
catfish whiskers.
And you would awaken
one half century later
to the screaming reel of now
feeling the swelling in your neck,
and the
oat cell cancer
schooling
in your lungs.

#1

Blight roots deep
cancer lesions gray matter
grasshoppers breeding.

Garden of dreamtime
and flowers gone to the bees,
then the black beetle.

The longnecked pilsner
I drank with you in springtime
an empty bottle.

THE GREAT DIVIDE

There's a warm wind blowing
through the woodland skies tonight.
My bones are tired and weary
I won't run—don't want to fight.
My pony stands restless
on these hills.
Connected to the land
she always will be.
There's a warm wind a-blowing
through the woodland skies tonight.

There was a time when the land
was a pure and peaceful place.
When bees came to the clover
and the land held God's own grace.
When you could drink from rivers
with the cup of your own hand.
Hear the deer running
in the shade of woodland stand.

A time when arm in arm
we were terraced with belief
in step with one another
in our joy and in our grief.
And there was dawn breaking
through the woodland trees beneath.

And the stars held out a beauty
in the blanket of the sky.
A dream for every dreamer,
A tear for every eye.
My pony could graze
without post or fence in sight
and with a warm wind blowing
through the woodland skies at night.

But now my pony

lifts her head into smoky air.
Her hooves paw the ground
and her nostrils flare.
What's in the wind
holds a blank and sterile stare
And my heart's spirit turns
under the woodland lawns, so fair.

Where can my children
ever call the stars by name?
Or know the sparkling waters
from where their life force came.

In that lonesome valley
where they must walk alone
what God will they talk to
if the earth has turned to stone.

Freedom is never free
it cost the changing of the heart.
If no one asks for it to stay
soon it will depart.
My voice may be a whisper
echoing in din
but the weight of being silent
is a mortal sin.

By my deeds I am written
and to them I will return.
How I'll be remembered
is by what I've earned.
And what I've done
for the sake of my children
and their kingdom come.

Now I cross the great divide.
The still small voice
of something, sounding deep inside.

For the sake of those who follow
I won't forget what's true.
Ride the foothills of my conscious
and do what I must do.

DRAGONFLY

A mosquito hawk
over my garden works
the foliage for insects.
The turret of her head
turns, tilts, swivels,
then up through the leaves
she goes vertical
to the hapless
"skeeter."
Some call her dragonfly,
but I do not because
I have seen the dragonfly
from jungle "dustoff"
bearing stretchers
out over the South China Sea
loaded with hapless
"skeeters."
We called these dragonflies,
"Sikorsky's Seconal"
rockets in proboscis,
fifty caliber machine guns
mounted in the thorax
spitting full metal jackets
over dead and wounded.
They worked the killing fields
in squadrons
and we worshipped them.
There is a low note
to piston-down-stroke
that even to this day
50 years distant
from the carnage of my youth
I can sense.
My heart beats
with the angry ache
of pistons
booming downward

rotating blade,
halfaturn- halfaturn-
halfaturn - halfaturn
about the approximately
vertical axis of my ears.
There is an air force base in Massachusetts
that they fly out of.
Their flight path
is above my garden.

Do they see me
peasant to my plants,
hoe in hand, squash underfoot?
There are the good ones
and the bad ones—cargo carriers
and gunships—there is no telling
by blade-down-beat
one from the other.
I must stare them out of the blue.
If you come to my garden
I can show you the mosquito hawk
her terrible beauty,
over basil, sage and thyme.

CHECK-OUT TIME

1987 Ramada Inn Air Crash and Fire and a friend's survival.

She smiled at the man
using the hotel lobby phone
as he raised his left index finger
in the air signing that he would be done
in a minute or two.
In exchange of glances
she indicated no hurry
for him to end his call
so she could make her
routine morning call-in
to the office and exited the hotel thinking;
Coffee first; a café a block away; then return
to make the call and checkout.
She gazed precipitately upward;
mundane scattered gray clouds
wore little chance of rain;
around her street traffic
was commonplace, humdrum,
unpretentious, bland; predictable
as an Indianapolis Tuesday.

Minutes later
a military plane
plummeted into the hotel;
cockpit and engine careening
into the lobby; jet fuel igniting upon impact;
Eight people incinerated instantly;
And one more, clothes burned off, holding
a melted phone in his charred right hand.

Time as an indigo child
in dye cast scrapbook
of remembering haunts
like all Hallows Eve.
She is dreaming now;

The man politely yields
the phone to her
in a hotel lobby;
and he goes off to the café.

A MOMENT OF SILENCE AND CUE-UP THE NEXT SONG

Death is
the end of the play list.
No failed vacuum tubes or transistors,
no tripped circuit breakers; engineers
stretching over schematics.
Options to call in,
complain, flatter, console, request,
disconnected, dissolved
in the wavelength of a heartbeat.
No hardware, software, human error—only
the stylus set in the eternity of the last groove
and the fact that the show has moved to
an unknown clear channel station
somewhere in the ambient static patter
of the universe—the sudden waking
to the ultimate commentator.
This is a radio world
with no segue but one;
a moment of silence
and cue-up the next song.

THE PANCAKE

...Isn't it funny Karamazov,
all this grief and pancakes afterward...
(Fyodor Mikhailovich Dostoevsky)

Let us have pancakes after grief,
baptized by boysenberry—butter as sunlight.
Pounds of pancakes. Pillars of pancakes.
Pancake palisades. Pancake precipice.
Bastions of battercake, fortress of flannel cake,
fields of flapjacks, griddlecake galaxies,
hotcake hinterlands—call barges of butter
to our ritual after grief—maple tankers
barreling down the interstate.

THINGS THAT CHANGE

Cool nights and mild sunny days make sweet grapes.
Good shoes can reshape the arches.
A small smile can change a big frown.

And we change—if we didn't, we'd be old crusty socks.
We'd be beef jerky whose double dose of preservatives
make us taste like cow chips.

What is the measure of all this change?
Sears doesn't sell a measuring cup
to pour our "daily did" or "nightly do" into.

Yet we can open a bottle of wine
and know the sun it took in.

We can take our shoes off, massage our feet
and soothe the steps of each new day.

We can smile and turn frowns around just for grins.

We can look around us and see
the character of heart of those we have been
through changes with and in that
take measure.

WILD CLOWNS

"Why don't bears eat clowns?" he asked me.
(His upper lip curling into smile)
I answered, "I don't know." And with a giggle he said,
"Because they taste funny! "
And I sat next to him taking his hand into mine;
"That's a great joke.
Can I make an observation?
Somewhere, someplace, sometime,
a bear must have licked a clown
to know that they taste funny.
And that must have been in a circus
because in all my days
I have never seen a clown in the woods.
And I have looked for them from Florida to Alaska
and never glimpsed red suspenders and yellow hair
leaping over underbrush, paddle footing away
in a honking rush to elude my camera.
It is said that the wild clown is extinct."
The lad gripped my hand tightly,
"Why did they die out?"
"I believe it was when people forgot
how to laugh and began to ridicule
the ridiculous as having no worth.
We pawned our hearts for merchandise
and being became a franchise, therapy, an industry.
Wild clowns eat joy and the world starved them out.
Time was when they use to roam in troupes
and appear at the outskirts of towns
to perform their slapstick. But laughter turned to chuckles
and chuckles to grins and grins to apathy.
And they wandered into the dark woods
with a painted tear on their cheeks.
No wild clown has been seen again.
But they may be alive
So here's what you must do:
Laugh as much as you can.
See the ridiculous in everything.

And each evening put your joy in a bowl
and leave it at the edge of the woods
and maybe, just maybe."

LOVELY IN YOUR DAYS

Who could be anyone but
you so lovely in your days.
Not one among the billions
could wear your smile,
or sing the way you sing.
Morning birds swoop down
to hear your whistle's early stroll.
When you are raised in thought,
the flag of your appeal surrenders doubt.
By your quiet smile
people go home to kiss their children.
The only thing you do too well is humbleness.
Go stand upon a high place
beneath the bowing clouds
and listen to yourself.

SKIPPING STONES

If you do a good one
it's one, two, three, four, five,
then the unseen spiral to the bottom
that no one
can make heads of tales out of—Well
except for one woman I know
who makes psychic claims
to the skip of stones
both in the way and number
of the side of surface against surface
and in the ripples
which she states
is our future
before we
bottom
out.
She claims the secret's in stone selection
and a level hand towards the point
where surface will suffice to carry.
If the Tarot, then why no stones?
Human nature is the deeper reading.
I believe she is accurate
about matters of the heart.
I'll say it is love,
but she puts a fuller spin on it.
And if you toss her for an answer
she says something so strange
that it sounds true.
She believes we are the stone
gone from the hand of what we were,
one, two, three, four, fiving it.
And that a good throw is a good life.

ROSARY OF CRUMBS

This morning as we ate bread
and drank sweet coffee
you did not seem to mind
the crumbs I left upon the sheet,
or my finger wet with saliva
that only hours ago
I had kissed you with
pushing down upon them
to bring them back to my lips.
You laughed—a red-bellied robin
hopping on a new mown lawn.
Birds were in your eyes,
the bed our aviary.
Maybe love looks like this.
Maybe it's a moment
then another, then another, then another
all connected together,
a rosary of crumbs.

WITHOUT YOUR LOVE

I woke up this morning
on the flotilla of my life
realizing that every step
has the possibility of
sudden drowning—of going
down clean out of sight
with the entire world
over my head.
My hat floating away
and folks asking;
"Where's Dan?"
And me bubbling up with
the little breath of what I know
in the peace and anger of what I am
back towards the light in your eyes;
your hand reaching out to me
ah friend,
what would
I do
without
your love?

WHERE EVERY BIRD SINGS

You are the place I go where every bird sings
A morning song before day begins.
In bird songs and dawn's alpenglow
I find the peace I long for.
Not that you are that peace or bird song
But in them I find my desire for you.
Not that you are anything I can say
Only that when I consider your light
I realize how long my night has been
And how deep.

RHAPSODY

That which is beautiful I know,
A sonata by Mozart,
a mobile by Calder,
a blues rift
lifted off the neck of Lucile,
by BB. King.
The three days in October
when there is no other word
for Southern New England
but pastel.
The list goes on like a Whitman poem.
Bubbles up in the ball jar
of my head after the harvest.
When the vacuum's set
the metal lid puckers in.
I know those beans will last.

So, beauty keeps me upright.
As movement is to bike riding
so, beauty is to balance.
It catches my wobble and
spins out from its hub,
Gravity.

Even so,
the child yesterday
carried on her mother's hip
reaching out her soft finger
and touching the condensation
upon my plastic milk jug
at the A&P
and the way she said "cold"
Her pure rhapsody,
masterful, timeless.

LOOKING FOR MAESTRO

Where has my song gone?

Have the somber faces
calculating numbers at the office
put my song into a spreadsheet?

The Bossa Nova of my joy
and romance been epilated
like a Brazilian bikini wax
strip, stick, and pull
without even a triangle.

Has the g-cleft of my score
sunk to a minor key?

Why is the lithe quarter note
not stepping up to measure.

Is the bassoon of my soul
lacking a double reed;
I blow and hear only
an oboe.

Where is my improvisation
and all that jazz?

The long-haired conductor
and the audience
 with a stand-up ovation
  roaring the
    BRAVO
      of creation?

GLASS PLATE

You sent me home
With a glass plate filled
With lasagna and some asparagus
Off to the side.
It was your gift and I was grateful
For the green and red odd couple—I've always
Had a place in my heart for primary colors.
What I loved more than
The food was the glass plate.
Like you, a one-of-a-kind glass plate
With bluing patina; an oblong
Circle of glass with a noticeable distortion,
Lacking any notion that it was made for a set.
Artful Yes!
I love the "is" of the plate.
The distortions I can view through it.
We all have a place setting
With a noticeable distortion
The opalescent colored glass of us;
The bread and butter of the soul;
Clean it and hold it up saying
Look at me through this.

HYMN AND HER

Porch music
Appalachian andante
several evenings
a week for 7 years
toting her guitar,
tuning it
E, A, D, G, B, E
in unison
with her
aging friend
tuning his;
remembering
old songs
under scores
of southern stars
Virginia
heavenly firmament.
Times tremolo
weaker and weaker
for the last two years
old strings
un-rocking rocker;
he passed.
She wisely says,

"… Just to be still
    and sit with the quiet
    for a while—healing is
    nestled somewhere
    in this quiet space.
    Allow the space it needs."

Finale.

NUMBERS

As a child
My kitchen had no walls
And everything ranged
In big bubbling pots of
Winter, spring, summer, autumn,
Peas, carrots, corncob days
Husked, rising to the surface
In the golden bullion of universal soup.
Numbers. Numbers. Numbers,
Numbers were something
I wanted more than anything.
Wanted ten shopping carts filled with ice cream;
Wanted sixteen cases of orange soda:
Wanted to be eighteen—then twenty-one;
Wanted five girlfriends
And two more for the weekend.
Wanted the power of numbers.
More was magic, majestic, and magnificent.
I never understood the numbers
In my parents' heart.
The endless trying
To make two plus two equal five.
Didn't know that numbers
Could numb and murder the soul.
That the Judas tree of numbers
Can have countless limbs
And still give no shade under the finite sun.

Now as a man of numbers
The weight of my ledger
Middling in years,
Thinning of hair
Records my loss and my gain
Realizing that love and life are singular.
Now I long for one true thought.
One poem that's brave enough to be.
One companion whom I can be infinite with.
One is so rare a number.

TO KEEP THE FAITH THAT IS HUMMINGBIRD

Red with sugared syrup my feeder's sweet sway
A Hummingbird comes to my porch.
Come hovers his hunger hardily stout of tongue
where I have hung my desire to see him.
He turns in moment of atmosphere
An acrobat on air trapeze.
The red crest of his throat makes a crusade.
A pod with wings sipping at the grail,
God's miracle of fierce smallness.

Shall my courage rise in knowing him/her
who has in his thousand-mile migration surrendered not!
Or in her solitude among great storms
Waited out the despair of clouds.
I pray for you and me
such small miracle of flight
And to keep the faith that is hummingbird.

ETERNITY AS AN EPITAPH

Between man and metaphor
Jesus played the hero.
Always popular at late night dinners with tax collectors
he quipped to his beloved,
"Sinners need me more than you do".
Something there is about a sinner dinner host
that knows a good party needs a designated driver.
Jesus' humor was biblical by invitation.
It goes back to the day Adam told Eve he ate from the tree of knowledge.
Eve said, "You're kidding me."

It would take thousands of years
for this dynamic obscure hilarity to be broadcast
on comedychannel.com.

If we have a vote in heaven
we should not elect saviors.
Heaven should be about good health care, schools, and the environment.
It should be about growing old with dignity.
And no one dying without
 a candle being
                lit
                        for
                                them.

56 FILBERT STREET

In this poem Eddie (5) years old is my great grandfather.

(In search of my great grandfather
Murry Federal Archives, Waltham, MA.)

He resides in microfiche
wound on a reel
in box labeled T-765-118.
He is 42 years old. A laborer.
His wife, Ophelia. Age 43,
keeps house
and their children
George, 21
Alick, 16
Salinia, 11
Sarah, 9
Frank, 7
Eddie, 5
Martin, 5
Katie, 1
list in a crowded house
on 56 Filbert street
in the town of Geddes, New York.

The year is 1880.
The clerk's black cursive
reaches across the years
scrawling a census of knowing
into the monocular scope
of insistent now.
Jacob, my great grandfather
stands at the front door.
He looks at me as I peer through the
yellowing page at him.
He speaks to me.
He knows who I am.

"You have come a long way to see me.
There is nothing much to show you here.
Your grandfather is sleeping,
I'll call for him."

He calls for Eddie.
Eddie comes and stands beside him.
He kneels down next to Eddie
and points up at me saying,

" This is the poet
that your son's son
has become.
You will be 76 years old
when Daniel will be born.
He has come to find us out
and put us in his book."

Eddie looks hesitantly up at me,
the brown green of his eyes
shining out of the yellowing-black and white ledger
like vivid pastel pigment chalked into
the gray slate of time's walkway.

"How do you know his name, father?"

And Jacob answers,

"I just know."

I want to tell Eddie
about the photographs I've seen of him.
A skin withered old man
sitting at an oak table
in the dilapidation of 90 years.
He is a Buffalo nickel in a changeless purse.
His brown-green eyes cast downward.
His large ears leaning for sound.
His huge hands grasping a glass of water.

But now
another picture
I see of him—mouth under
a cast iron pour spout,
his right hand pulling down upon
a long-handled pump
at the common well
in village dust
and gas-lit street.
He peers into a dusty sky
listening to
the staved chatter
of oaken days.
And I do not speak
for sake of circumstance
and time's irascibility.
Eddie smiles and turns
vanishing into the house.
I ask Jacob,

"What about you and the others?"

Jacob says,

"I've come a long way from Baden Germany.
America is 56 Filbert Street.
Ophelia has her hands full.
There is nothing more
this paper will allow me
to give you.
If there is poetry in this
then take it."

YOUR LIFE MATTERS

When you have survived
a certain number of years
authenticity matters;
adaptation under gravity's effect
is being true to oneself.
Start living life
honestly,
your
masterpiece
is
waiting.

GET BUSY SONS AND DAUGHTERS ALL

Get busy sons and daughters all
as days are short and years are small.
Times adze dresses and unsquares
haves, and have-nots, and timber bares.
Get busy now before your end.
The saddest words are,
"I could have been."

I rode a bee when I was three
or did the bee ride me?
Oh, I guess it was the genesis
of all my poetry.

CPSIA information can be obtained
at www.ICGtesting.com
Printed in the USA
BVHW041228210222
629667BV00014B/703